FIRST AMERICANS

The Mandan

TERRY ALLAN HICKS

Marshall Cavendish
Benchmark
New York

ACKNOWLEDGMENTS

For Nancy, who makes everything possible

Series consultant: Raymond Bial

The craft on pages 20–21 was adapted from Marian Broida's *Projects About the Plains Indians* (Marshall Cavendish, 2004).

Marshall Cavendish Benchmark
99 White Plains Road
Tarrytown, New York 10591
www.marshallcavendish.us

Library of Congress Cataloging-in-Publication Data
Hicks, Terry Allan.
The Mandan / by Terry Allan Hicks.
p. cm. -- (First Americans)
Summary: "Provides comprehensive information on the background, lifestyle,
beliefs, and present-day lives of the Mandan people"--Provided by publisher.
Includes bibliographical references and index.
ISBN 978-0-7614-4130-4
1. Mandan Indians--Juvenile literature. I. Title.
E99.M2H53 2010
978.004'9752--dc22
2008028367

Front cover: A girl in a traditional beaded and tanned dress poses on the Fort Berthold Indian Reservation in North Dakota.
Title page: The seal of the Fort Laramie Treaty
Photo research by: Connie Gardner
Cover photo by Marilyn "Angel" Wynn/Nativestock.com
The photographs in this book are used by permission and through the courtesy of: Nativestock.com: Marilyn Angel Wynn, 1, 7, 9, 17, 22, 39; Alamy: Tom Salver, 4; Interfoto Pressebildagentur, 6, 26, 32; Visual Arts Library, 29; The Image Works: Mary Evans Picture Library, 12, 24; Stapleton Collection, 14; Roger Viollet, 12; AP Photo: Eloise Ogden, 41; Corbis: Minnesota Historical Society, 36; Tom Bean Photography: 37; Raymond Bial: 16, 31.

Editor: Deborah Grahame
Publisher: Michelle Bisson
Art Director: Anahid Hamparian
Series Designer: Symon Chow

Printed in Malaysia
1 3 5 6 4 2

CONTENTS

1 · WHO ARE THE MANDAN?

For thousands of years, Native American peoples have lived on the northern plains, in present-day North and South Dakota. Most of them led a **nomadic** existence, following the herds of **bison** that they hunted. But some, like the Mandan (MAN-dan), were **sedentary** peoples, who lived in one place, building lasting villages and relationships with their neighbors. The Mandan, a **Siouan** people, were among the bravest warriors on the plains, but they usually fought only to defend themselves. Their peaceful, welcoming ways placed them at the center of life on the plains for centuries.

The word *Mandan* means "people who live by the river." The Mandan's history is linked with the great river that we know today as the Missouri, and two smaller rivers, the Heart and the Knife, that flow into it. The Mandan crossed the

The rivers of the northern plains have always played an essential role in Mandan life.

A nineteenth-century engraving shows Mandan using their bull boats on the river.

rivers in **bull boats** made of bison hide, to catch fish and trade with their neighbors. They also farmed along the rivers' banks. They grew a small, tough type of corn that kept well through the winter. This corn was ideally suited to the short northern growing season, and it made the Mandan very important to their neighbors.

The Mandan and their neighbors depended on corn for their survival.

Every fall, after the corn harvest, the other peoples of the plains traveled great distances to trade dried meat, animal skins, cooking pots, weapons, and, in later years, horses, in exchange for corn. Even the Mandan's traditional enemies, including the warlike Teton Sioux, set aside their differences so that they would have enough food for the long, cold winter to come.

The Mandan, like all Native Americans, are the descendants of prehistoric peoples who **migrated** across a "land bridge" that once connected Asia and the Americas, perhaps as long ago as 100,000 BCE. Very little is known about the earliest Mandan, but they may have lived in the Ohio River Valley, more than 1,000 miles (1,600 kilometers) southeast of their present-day home. Sometime around 1000 CE, the Mandan were living along the southern reaches of the Missouri River. Beginning about 1150 they began to move northward. By the early 1600s the Mandan were living along the upper Missouri. Two other sedentary tribes, the Hidatsa and the Arikara, also lived in this area. It was here that European and American **explorers** and **settlers** came to know and admire the Mandan.

The first Europeans to encounter the Mandan were fur traders led by a French-Canadian soldier and explorer named Pierre Gaultier de Varennes, Sieur de la Vérendrye, in 1724. La Vérendrye wrote that the Mandan were well known for

The remains of early Mandan and Hidatsa villages can still be seen today.

being a generous people, saying that they "feed liberally all who came among them. . . ." More French and then British traders followed, sometimes living in the Mandan's villages.

Lewis and Clark Meet the Mandan

The Mandan's hospitality helped ensure the success of one of the most important ventures in the history of the United States: the Lewis and Clark expedition. President Thomas Jefferson had sent the expedition on a long journey across the continent, to explore and map the vast, "unknown" tract of land that the United States had recently purchased from France. Lewis and Clark entered Mandan territory in late October 1804, just as an early snow was falling. Two Mandan village chiefs—Sheheke ("Big White") and Black Cat—welcomed them, and gave them food, a place to stay through the long, hard winter that followed, and valuable information. They also introduced Lewis and Clark to a French-Canadian fur trapper and his sixteen-year-old Shoshone wife, Sacagawea, who became their guides. If not for the Mandan's hospitality, the expedition would probably have failed, and the explorers might not even have survived.

The Mandan did not have a written language until modern times, so they passed on their history, their beliefs, and their stories in different ways. One of the ways the Mandan preserved their stories was by painting on bison hides. The Lewis and Clark expedition sent "1 Buffalow robe painted by a Mandan man representing a battle which was faught 8 years since" back to Washington, D.C.

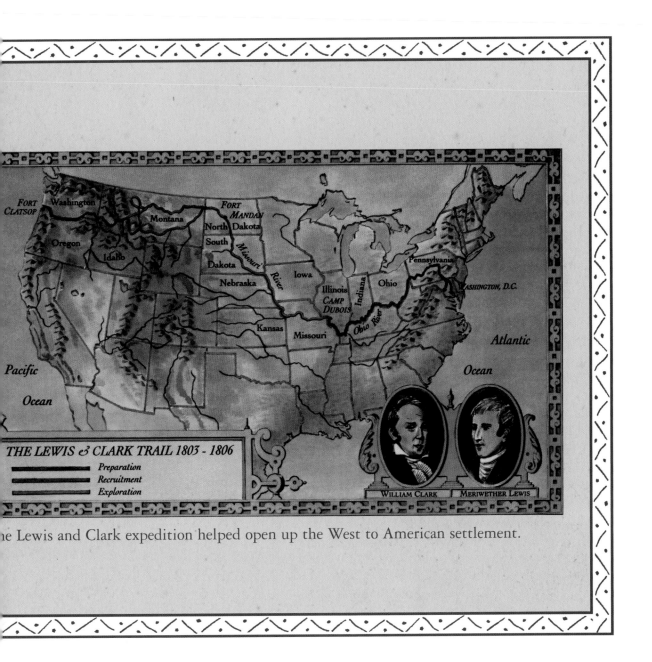

The Lewis and Clark expedition helped open up the West to American settlement.

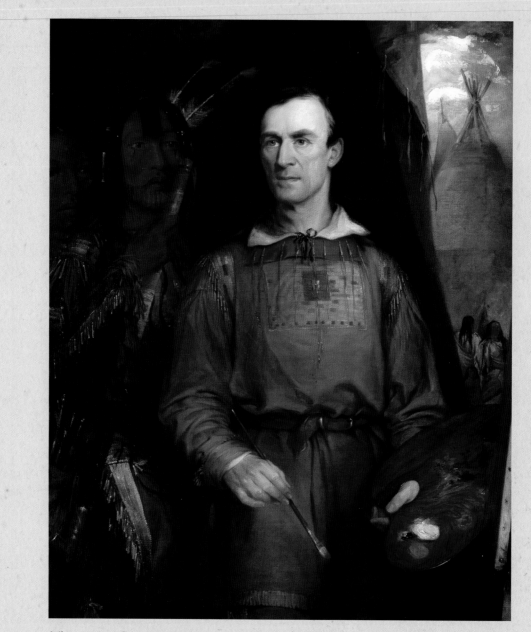

The artist George Catlin painted Native Americans during his travels across the West.

These encounters helped both the Mandan and their European and American visitors. In the years that followed, many more visitors came to Mandan territory. Merchants and traders continued to bring goods that the Mandan needed. Beginning in the 1740s they brought horses, which allowed the Mandan to travel much greater distances. In the 1830s two talented artists, George Catlin and Karl Bodner, also traveled across the plains. They created detailed paintings showing Mandan life in those days.

In time, the encounters between the new arrivals and the Mandan began to threaten the Mandan's way of life—and their very existence.

2 · LIFE ON THE NORTHERN PLAINS

The Mandan's homeland is a difficult place to live, with long, harsh winters and little rainfall. But the Mandan made the most of their environment, especially the rivers. They trapped catfish, sturgeon, and other fish, and gathered mussels. The land along the rivers' banks was made rich and fertile by the spring floods. Unlike many other Plains Indians, the Mandan were farmers, growing beans, squash, sunflowers, tobacco, and their precious corn. They cut down trees, including willow, cottonwood, oak, and box elder, for firewood and to build their villages on the high ground, away from the floods.

By the time Europeans and Americans began to arrive, a Mandan village was made up of a group of twenty to a hundred earth **lodges**, often circled by a protective wall made of sharpened stakes. Each lodge was home to as many as forty members

A Native American village in winter, painted by Karl Bodmer

Nothing was more important to a Mandan clan than its sacred bundle.

of a **clan**. A Mandan lodge was dome-shaped, with a wooden-frame entrance, and was covered with earth. Part of the lodge was underground, so it was warm in winter and cool in summer. In the center of the roof there was a square smoke hole for a cooking fire, a central area for working and eating, and raised sleeping platforms. At the entrance to the lodge was any Mandan's most precious possession: the sacred bundle. This was a bag that contained articles—for example, seed corn or eagle feathers—with religious meaning. The contents of the sacred bundle were a secret, known only to the person, family, or clan that owned it.

The lodges were clustered in a rough circle around a large open area. The wealthiest and most influential clans lived closest to this area, which was used for religious rituals, dances, and games. A **medicine lodge** sat at the north side of

The entrance to a Mandan medicine lodge

the open area. In the middle of the circle was a painted wooden pole, called the Big Canoe, which was the **symbol** of an important god called Lone Man.

The Mandan were skilled craftspeople who made beautiful beaded moccasins, painted animal-skin robes, and cooking utensils made from fired clay or animal bones.

A Mandan village had two chiefs, one for war and another for peace. They were always men, but women played an important role in Mandan life. They tended the riverside gardens where the Mandan's corn, beans, squash, sunflowers, and pumpkins grew. They also did most of the work of building the earth lodges in which their clans lived. At different times of the year, the women went out into the surrounding areas—accompanied by the village children—to gather wild fruit, including buffalo berries, chokecherries, plums, and grapes. Mandan women had great influence within the village, as well. A lodge actually belonged to the woman who was head of the family or clan.

Great Plains Stew

Corn, beans, and squash were important foods for the Mandan and their neighbors. This simple, hearty stew—based on a traditional recipe—uses all three. If you substitute field corn or hominy for the sweet corn, the recipe will be close to what the Mandan used. You should ask an adult to help cut up the ingredients and turn on the stove.

Ingredients

- 3 green onions
- 1/2 acorn or butternut squash
- 1/4 teaspoon (1.25 grams) thyme
- 2 tablespoons (10 g) butter
- 1 cup (150 g) fresh or frozen corn (if fresh, use two ears of corn)
- 1 cup (150 g) canned white beans (for example, great northern or cannelloni)
- 1/2 cup (240 milliliters) milk
- 1/2 cup (240 ml) water
- 1 cube vegetable bouillon
- Salt and pepper to taste

Cut the green onions into thin slices. Peel the squash and cut it into one-inch-square pieces. Place the butter in a large saucepan, and cook the green onions and squash over medium heat for about five minutes. Stir in the corn and beans, then add the thyme. Add the milk, water, and vegetable bouillon, being careful not to splash the hot mixture. Reduce the heat to low, and simmer for about 15 minutes. Add salt and pepper, if you like, then serve.

Make a Bull Boat

A Mandan bull boat was made by stretching a fresh (undried) bison hide over a circular frame of bent willow branches. (The hide had to be from a male bison or "bull.") A long wooden paddle was then tied to the side of the boat. Why not try making a model of a bull boat, using easy-to-find materials? You may want to ask an adult to help.

You will need:

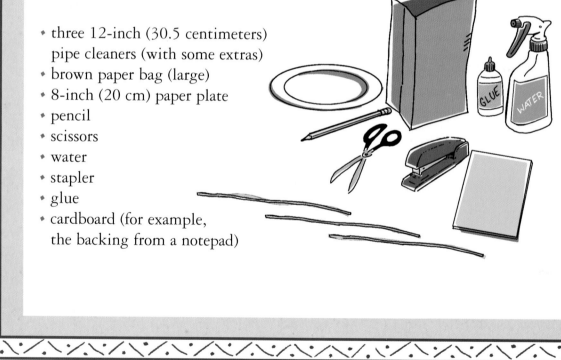

- three 12-inch (30.5 centimeters) pipe cleaners (with some extras)
- brown paper bag (large)
- 8-inch (20 cm) paper plate
- pencil
- scissors
- water
- stapler
- glue
- cardboard (for example, the backing from a notepad)

1. Form one pipe cleaner into a circle, fastening the ends together. Cut the other pipe cleaners into halves.

2. Fasten two ends at the top of the circle, about one inch apart. Fasten the other ends to the bottom of the circle.

3. Take two more pipe cleaner halves and fasten them at one of the sides of the circle. "Weave" them through the first halves, going over and under, then fasten them on the other side of the circle. Gently push down on the woven-together halves until a bowl shape appears.

4. Place the paper plate over the paper bag, trace over it, and cut out the circle. Crumple up the paper circle, sprinkle it with water, uncrumple it, and place the pipe cleaner frame on it.

5. Wrap the wet paper around the frame, folding any extra paper over the top.

6. Staple the paper all around the circle, and cut away the extra paper. (If there are any torn papers, you can fix them by gluing on bits of the leftover paper from the bag.)

7. Cut a paddle out of the cardboard.

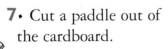

A mother and daughter in traditional dress on the Fort Berthold Reservation

When a young man married, he went to live in his bride's family's lodge, to become part of her clan.

The men were responsible for protecting the village against attacks by other Native American peoples—a constant threat on the plains. They were the hunters, traveling into the high country beyond the villages in search of deer, elk, and antelope. Most of all, they hunted bison, for both its meat and its hide. The Mandan thought the best-tasting food of all was the rotten meat of drowned bison. A rare white

Native Americans are shown hunting bison in this nineteenth-century painting by George Catlin.

Mandan gather for horse races in the 1830s.

bison hide was one of the most valuable things a Mandan could own, because he could not become a chief if he did not own one.

Even for this peaceful farming people, hunting and fighting abilities were essential. A Mandan man could only become a chief if he had proved himself in battle. (He also had to show his generosity by giving away many things of value.) This is why many of the games that the Mandan played in their villages helped them sharpen the skills they needed to survive in an often-hostile world. Mandan men competed in foot races, horse races, and archery contests. Women played a game in which they bounced a leather ball from their foot to their knee. And everyone in the village competed to throw spears at a ball or ring rolling across the ground.

3 · MANDAN BELIEFS

The Mandan worshipped many **deities**, or gods, including Old Woman Who Never Dies, a powerful spirit who lived on the moon. She had many children, including Day, Night, the Sun, and the Morning Star.

The Mandan believed that every human being had four different souls, which went to different places after death, as well as an animal spirit that lived within him or her. They often kept objects associated with these animals—such as eagle feathers—in their sacred bundles. The Mandan thought that many animals had special powers. They often kept owls, for example, because they believed owls could tell the future.

The Mandan prayed to these spirits, and many others, throughout the day. A prayer could be a simple offering of food, or a complex religious ritual that lasted many days. The

The Mandan used symbols to represent their deities, such as Sun and Moon (shown here).

most important ritual in Mandan life was the Okipa ceremony, held every summer. This ritual marked the time when a boy reached adulthood. The Mandan believed that suffering made them stronger and pleased the deities. Young children were sometimes encouraged to **fast**—and even to torture themselves, sometimes by cutting off part of a finger—to prove themselves worthy.

To prepare for the Okipa, a Mandan boy would fast for days. Then, when he was weakened by hunger, bone needles were passed through the skin of his chest, and he was hung by leather straps from the roof of the medicine lodge, sometimes for days. This agonizingly painful ritual brought him visions of the spirits that would live inside him and guide him for the rest of his life. When he was finally cut down, exhausted, dazed, and bleeding, he was no longer a boy. He was a man.

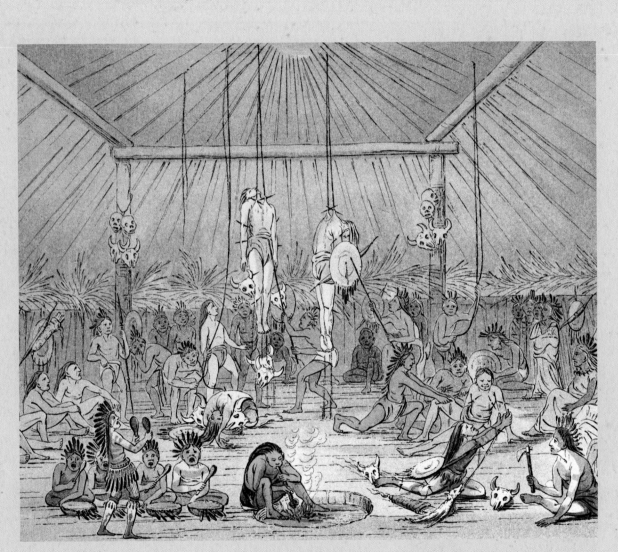

The Okipa ritual was the most important moment in a Mandan man's life.

First Creator and Lone Man

The Mandan had several different stories about the creation of the world and the Mandan people. In one story, two rival deities created two worlds, separated by the Missouri River. First Creator made the hills and valleys south of the Missouri, as well as bison, deer, and snakes. Lone Man created the plains north of the river, as well as birds and fish—and human beings. Lone Man was later reborn as a Mandan himself. He was the deity who probably meant the most to the Mandan, and he taught them many useful skills, such as hunting and making fire. The first Mandan are said to have lived by the shores of a great underground lake. They climbed up a grapevine and discovered the world above. The vine snapped, and half of the Mandan fell, to be trapped underground forever.

4 · A CHANGING WORLD

By the beginning of the nineteenth century, the Mandan were living in prosperous villages near the site of the present-day city of Mandan, North Dakota. But the arrival of more outsiders was about to bring a series of devastating blows.

In 1837 an **epidemic** of smallpox, a deadly and highly **contagious** disease, broke out. The Mandan, like many Native American peoples, had no natural resistance to "white men's diseases." By the time the epidemic ended the following year, more than a thousand Mandan were dead—and perhaps as few as 125 remained alive. The Mandan felt great bitterness toward the newcomers who had brought the disease. As he lay dying, the Mandan chief Four Bears called them "a set of Black harted Dogs," saying, "they have deceived Me, them that I always considered as Brothers, has turned Out to be My Worst enemies."

The Mandan's traditional medicine could not protect them against new diseases.

The Mandan were so badly weakened that they had no choice but to join forces with the Hidatsa, who had also suffered terribly. Together the two peoples moved to Like-a-Fishhook-Village, a settlement near the trading post of Fort Berthold in the western part of North Dakota, in 1845. The U.S. government made many promises to the Mandan in the years that followed—and broke almost all of them. The 1851 Treaty of Fort Laramie set aside a huge tract of land for a reservation for the Mandan and the Hidatsa. In 1862 the Arikara agreed to join them there.

The Fort Berthold Reservation was created in 1870, with a total of more than 13 million acres (5.2 million hectares) set aside for the three peoples. The Mandan, Hidatsa, and Arikara finally had a home of their own again. But their rights were never respected. In 1890 the U.S. government simply gave most of the southern half of the reservation to a company that was laying railroad tracks across the West. In 1910 a large section of the northeastern part of the reservation was stolen by settlers. By this time, just forty years after the creation of

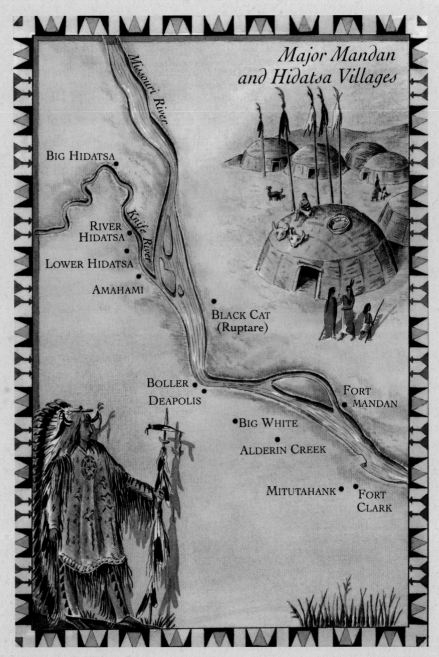

Major Mandan
and Hidatsa Villages

Missouri River

Big Hidatsa

Knife River

River
Hidatsa

Lower Hidatsa

Amahami

Black Cat
(Ruptare)

Boller
Deapolis

Fort
Mandan

Big White

Alderin Creek

Mitutahank

Fort
Clark

For hundreds of years, the Mandan made their home along the Missouri
River and other rivers that branched through the North Dakota prairies.

Railroads brought new settlers to the West, threatening the Native Americans' way of life.

the reservation, it had shrunk to 900,000 acres (364,000 hectares), less than a tenth of what had been promised. The suffering of the Mandan, Hidatsa, and Arikara—who formally joined together in 1934 as the Three Affiliated Tribes— was far from over.

In 1948 the federal government forced the people of the

Lake Sakakawea's beauty draws tourists to North Dakota today for fishing and boating.

reservation to sell yet another huge section of their land, so that the U.S. Army Corps of Engineers could build a dam and reservoir. By the time the project was completed, in 1954, a huge artificially created lake—Lake Sakakawea, named for Sacagawea, the guide the Mandan had introduced to Lewis and Clark—covered hundreds of homes and farms and forced their residents to move. The people had to live in unfamiliar communities, such as the aptly named New Town, that were isolated and difficult to reach. Many of the ties between communities, clans, and families were broken, perhaps forever.

One of the most important things that hold any people together is language—and the Mandan language was in danger of disappearing completely. By the 1990s only six fluent Mandan speakers remained, and it is possible that only one truly fluent Mandan speaker—an elderly rancher named Edwin Benson—is alive today. Fortunately for the Mandan, and for the rest of us, he works tirelessly with a California linguist, telling the old stories and helping to keep this precious language alive. Just as important, many younger Mandan are learning their native tongue, which is now taught in some reservation schools.

There are other signs of improvement and progress for the Three Affiliated Tribes, including the 1993 founding of a casino and resort hotel at the edge of Lake Sakakawea. This brought badly needed jobs and money to the reservation, but

Children on the Fort Berthold Reservation playing a traditional game

the social problems found on many reservations—poverty, unemployment, and alcoholism—still remain.

The twenty-first century brought another change to the reservation: the completion, in 2005, of the Four Bears Bridge. The bridge is named for the Mandan chief who died in the smallpox epidemic of 1836–1837, and crosses the Missouri River near New Town. The Three Affiliated Tribes hope that

The Mandan Language

The Mandan language belongs to the Siouan family, which includes the languages of peoples who live across a huge stretch of the central United States and Canada, as far north as the province of Alberta and as far south as the state of Mississippi. The Mandan language is most closely related to the Hidatsa and Crow languages. It is very complicated, with three different dialects, and it is very difficult to pronounce. Here are a few examples of common words:

English	Mandan
bald eagle	*patake*
boy	*suknumank*
cloud	*haade*
friend	*manuka*
girl	*sukmihe*
hand	*onka*
horse	*meniss*
man	*umank*
water	*mini*
woman	*mihe*

the bridge, which is decorated with images that celebrate their rich cultures, will help to reconnect people and families who have been separated by the flooding that created Lake Sakakawea, and link the proud pasts of the Mandan, Hidatsa, and Arikara with a brighter future.

The new Four Bears Bridge (shown here under construction in 2004) is helping to bring the Three Affiliated Tribes together.

· TIME LINE

The first Native Americans begin to migrate across a "land bridge" connecting Asia and North America.

The Mandan are living in the forests along the lower Missouri River.

The Mandan have settled in the upper Missouri Valley, where the Missouri meets the Knife and Heart rivers.

The first Europeans to meet the Mandan, led by the French-Canadian explorer La Vérendrye, enter Mandan territory.

The explorers of the Lewis and Clark expedition spend the winter with the Mandan and Hidatsa.

c. 20,000–100,000   c. 1000   c. 1600   1738   1804–1805

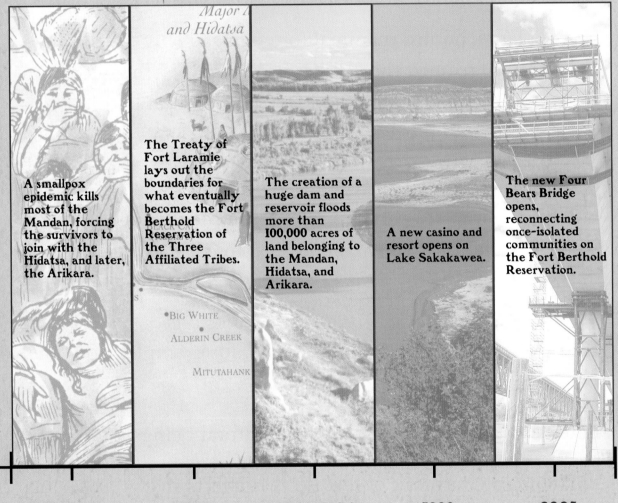

A smallpox epidemic kills most of the Mandan, forcing the survivors to join with the Hidatsa, and later, the Arikara.

The Treaty of Fort Laramie lays out the boundaries for what eventually becomes the Fort Berthold Reservation of the Three Affiliated Tribes.

The creation of a huge dam and reservoir floods more than 100,000 acres of land belonging to the Mandan, Hidatsa, and Arikara.

A new casino and resort opens on Lake Sakakawea.

The new Four Bears Bridge opens, reconnecting once-isolated communities on the Fort Berthold Reservation.

1836–1837   1851   1948–1954   1993   2005

· GLOSSARY

bison: a large, horned mammal (often mistakenly called buffalo) that once roamed the northern plains of North America in great numbers and was hunted for both its meat and its hide. (Buffalo are distantly related to bison and live in Europe, Asia, and parts of Africa.)

bull boats: circular boats, made of bison hide stretched over a wooden frame, that the Mandan used for river travel.

clan: a large "extended family."

contagious: easily spread (as a disease, for example) from one person to another.

deities: gods, spirits, or other supernatural beings.

epidemic: an outbreak of disease that affects many people in a short period of time.

explorers: people who travel to discover previously unknown places.

fast: to deliberately go without food.

lodges: permanent dwelling places built by some Native Americans.

medicine lodge: a structure where religious ceremonies are performed.

migrated: moved from one part of the world to another.

nomadic: moving from place to place.

sedentary: leading a settled way of life in one place.

settlers: people who move to a new place to live permanently.

Siouan: a large group of Native American peoples, and the languages they speak.

symbol: something that represents something else (for example, a statue representing a god).

Books

Broida, Marian. *Projects About the Plains Indians.* New York: Marshall Cavendish/Benchmark, 2004.

DeKeyser, Stacy. *Sacagawea.* (Watts Library Explorers). Danbury, CT: Franklin Watts, 2004.

Fradin, Dennis Brindell. *The Lewis and Clark Expedition.* New York: Marshall Cavendish/Benchmark, 2007.

Web Sites

Knife River Indian Villages
www.nps.gov/knri

Lewis and Clark: The Native Americans:
The Mandan Indians
www.pbs.org/lewisandclark/native/man.html

MHA Nation Three Affiliated Tribes: History:
The Mandan
www.mhanation.com/main/history/history_mandan.html

About the Author

Terry Allan Hicks has written more than a dozen titles for Benchmark Books, including a First Americans book about the Chumash people of the California coast. He lives in Connecticut with his wife, Nancy, and their three sons, Jamie, Jack, and Andrew.

· INDEX

Page numbers in **boldface** are illustrations.